HOPE FOR PAWS
Animal Rescue Organization

"When I look into the eyes of an animal I do not see an animal. I see a living being. I see a friend. I see a soul."
A.D. Williams

Hope For Paws is a non-profit rescue servicing Los Angeles and Southern California. It was founded in 2008 by Eldad Hagar and his then wife Audrey. Their dream was to bring second chances to all the forgotten animals living on the streets. Hope For Paws has traveled all over Southern California and beyond to Florida as well as many visits to Costa Rica. Eldad's secret to a successful rescue is patience. He takes as much time as needed to earn the animal's trust, making it as little traumatizing as possible for the animal in need. His secret weapons consist of the Hope For Paws lucky leash and a tasty cheeseburger. Thanks to the donations of people like yourselves, each animal is giving extensive medical treatment, groomed, and spayed or neutered. After the animal has been giving a clean bill of health they are then sent to a foster home while they await their loving forever homes. Team members such as Lisa Arturo and many others have helped Eldad to successfully save thousands of suffering animals off the streets and out of kill shelters. Hope For Paws would like to thank their donors for many years of help, love and support.

Please join Hope For Paws on 20 of their most successful rescues. Each Dog has its own short story about where they started, and where these beautiful dogs ended up. The second page consists of a collage celebrating the animal's journey and concluding with a beautiful portrait of each rescue dog for you to color. Some of the photos may be disturbing for certain viewers, but each and every story has a happy ending. Snuggle up in your favorite chair with your fur babies, and journey into this coloring keepsake book on an adventure of hope, love, and miracles.

Eldad, Lisa, and the rest of the Hope For Paws team would like to thank you all for years of supporting our cause.

I wish to dedicate this book to my beautiful children Autumn and Aaron. To my family, it is your love that drives me to bring beauty into this world as you have done to mine, I love you all.

With much love, Bonnie Mulchahey - Author and Artist

About the Author/Artist

My name is Bonnie Mulchahey. A few months ago I reached out to Hope For Paws and asked them if I would be able to create a coloring book inspired by their rescue stories. To my surprise, I received a call back from Lisa Arturo, Eldad's second in command. They were thrilled at the idea, and I went right to work on making this book. After months of hard work and dedication with the help from Lisa and Eldad, my dream finally became a reality. The majority of the book sales will go to Hope For Paws so that they may help more animals like these 20 dogs. I personally want to thank each and everyone of you for your contribution. I also wish to thank my good friend Sarah Rowan for all of her help in editing each story, as well as all of her encouragement in the making of this book.

Thousands of homeless dogs wander the streets in need of our help. There are also many more in high kill shelters who are destined for euthanization because they are too old, not attractive enough, or deemed too aggressive for adoption. Thousands of years of breeding has brought our canine friends closer to us. They are loyal, sweet and live for our love and approval. I encourage you before you before visiting a pet store or breeder, stop by your local pound. From personal experience I can tell you that a shelter dog who has been given a second chance at life will be the most grateful companion imaginable.

In 2008 I visited the San Bernardino animal pound in California. Inside a small kennel were 8 tiny dogs. There was a lonely black Chihuahua hiding in the corner who caught my eye. I asked the attendant to get her for me. She walked right up to the attendant, and he scooped her up. I took her into my arms and it was love at first sight for the both of us. She laid her head upon my chest, and the rest was history. I paid her adoption/ spay fee. Having to leave her there for one more night devastated me. The next day I waited by the phone worried that the vet would call and tell me that she had Parvo or maybe something even worse. I could not pick her up until 5pm after her Spaying. At 4pm I hopped in my car and rushed straight down to the vet. The nurse informed me that there was complications and asked me to wait inside of a room. I was terrified. How could I lose my love before I even got to know her? The door opened and the nurse walked in carrying my dog. She jumped 4 feet out of the nurses arms and ran onto my lap. The entire clinic was in shock that I had only just met this creature the day before. It was as if I raised her from a puppy. Unfortunately, she could not be spayed because she was severely underweight. They were also concerned that she was favoring her front paw. Apparently her leg had previously been broken. It was never taken care of so it set back improperly. Well, I just watched her jump from a high height so I was fairly certain that she was going to be okay. They offered to reimburse my money and send her back to the pound. I told them I would take my chances. I named her Squeek because she made this adorable little....well, Squeaking noise. As we walked into her new home she lept from my arms and raced around the house. For 7 years Squeek was my shadow. Everywhere I went she followed me, and If I left the house she crawled inside my backpack accompanying. When I had my children she would ride in the basket of the baby stroller. In February of 2016 Squeek became very ill. There was nothing I could do to save her. She will forever be my heart, and not a day goes by that I do not think about her cute smile.

I wish to dedicate this book to my beautiful children Autumn and Aaron - It is your love that makes it all worthwhile. To my sweet rescue fur baby Squeek and to my family, for all the years of encouragement in my talents and endeavors, I love you all.

With much love, Bonnie Mulchahey

Angelica - The lost angel

For over a month the groundskeepers at a remote cemetery outside of Los Angeles looked after an abandoned senior Corgi mix until a good Samaritan called Hope For Paws for help. Her previous owners had dumped her off perhaps because of her age, which is not uncommon for senior dogs to have this happen. Lisa Arturo and Eldad headed right down to save the little angel. It took some time to spot Angelica in the huge cemetery. At first Angelica was spooked by her rescuers, but some kind words and tasty hot dogs earned her trust. Angelica finally got close enough so that Lisa could grab her with the gentle snare. Angelica immediately surrendered into the loving arms of her new friends, letting Lisa place the Hope For Paws lucky leash around her neck. You could see the relief in Angelica's eyes. From the time they spotted her it took seven minutes to get Angelica in their car and onward to a new happy life. After being alone for so long and abandoned Angelica was so excited and thankful to finally be held once again.

At the vet, she received everything she required. She was bathed in warm water to wash away the fleas and pain. Then giving medication, immunizations, and all the food and water she could hope for.

Angelica went on to her new foster home at "Rescue From the Hart." She is such a loving dog and very laid back. Angelica still has some of that puppy power in her when she wants to play.

We all think that puppies are one of the most adorable creatures on this planet. Sadly, a lot of times people will discard older dogs once they have hit their golden years. Whether it be because they cannot afford the extra medical care that an elderly dog requires. Even more disheartening, just because they want a new puppy to play with. There are so many senior dogs in shelters that just want to be loved again. If you are looking for a new family member try considering an older dog. They just want to be loved like puppies too, and the best part is, they are already trained!

"Are you here to help me?"

Onward to a new life

Such a diva

What a beautiful smile.

Angelo – The tiny puppy with a big heart

Hope For Paws received a call about a small Chihuahua puppy living in a dirty ditch next to a biohazard disposal company. At first sight Angelo was excited to see Lisa Chiarelli and Eldad, but became spooked and ran into a deep trench between two walls making it very difficult to get to him. Losing sunlight, they decided to come back the next day and try again, this time they stood at separate ends of Angelo's hiding place that confined him. The trench was skinny and filled with weeds, cobwebs, spiders, branches, and the air was very thick with dust, making even more difficult to reach Angelo. He was terrified and tried everything he could to escape Eldad's gentle snare, he even tried climbing the walls and charging at Eldad. Eventually they were able to bribe him with treats and kind words. He finally realized they were there to help and calmed down allowing Lisa to hold him. Angelo was filthy, covered in cobwebs, fleas and dirt, but soon his life would change for the better, now that the Hope For Paws lucky leash was placed upon him. It took some careful movements and a ladder to get both Eldad and Angelo out of the trench, but soon they were on their way to the vet to get Angelo his medical care and a nice warm bath.

Eldad washed away all the remnants of Angelo's previous life on the streets and began teaching him about friendship. A few days later Angelo went to his foster home and met his new family and pack. He learned what it meant to be loved.

Angelo is blissful in the arms of his new friends.

Always check for a micro chip.

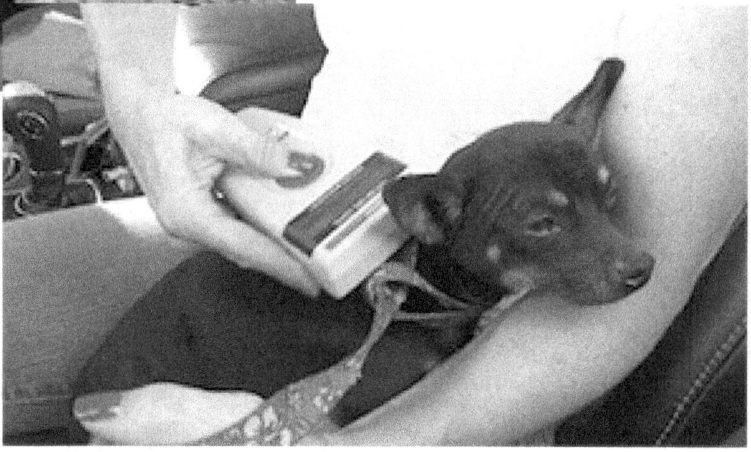

"I'm ready for my close up."

"Whatcha doing?"

Benji- The Frightened One

Hope For Paws received a call about a homeless 3 year old Lhasa apso mix, who had been living on the streets his whole life. As Eldad pulled up he found Benji lying underneath a pickup truck. Panting from the southern California summer, his overly matted fur was making him overheat and dehydrate. Hope For Paws was told that he was terrified of humans and would not let anyone near him. Out of fear Benji took off towards a busy intersection. Eldad was forced to grab the gentle snare and run after him. This would be no easy rescue. Luckily Benji ran into a neighbor's driveway with a gate and Eldad managed to confine him inside. Quickly he latched the gate before Benji could bolt back out into the street. The terrified puppy freaked out, spinning around and biting the leash. The struggle caused some damage to Benji's mouth as he chewed on the snare. Having never known a loving touch in his life it was hard for Benji to trust Eldad and Lisa Chiarelli. Benji finally calmed down and let them pet him. It did not take long for Benji to understand that Eldad and Lisa were only there to help. Lisa placed the lucky Hope For Paws leash around Benji's neck and they headed to the vet. Benji curled up inside the car, understanding that his trying life on the street was now over. He seemed to be grateful for the warmth and compassion that his rescuers were giving him.

At the vet, it was time to shave away a lifetime of neglect. It took almost three hours to remove all of Benji's matts, only to reveal severe skin damage, and a massive flea and mite infestation. After a warm medicated bath and flea dip Lisa began working to heal Benji's soul. She cuddled him, a feeling he had never known before.

Lisa took Benji home and spent over ten days trying to get through to him, but he was shut down emotionally. It took the love of Lola and Frankie, Lisa's dogs, to help bring Benji out of his shell. Finally, they saw a real dog emerge as he played and cuddled with his new fur friends. Today Benji is enjoying his forever loving home and has a whole new attitude towards the world around him thanks to the efforts of Hope For Paws.

Scared and alone no longer.

Time for you make over.

Let's go home Benji.

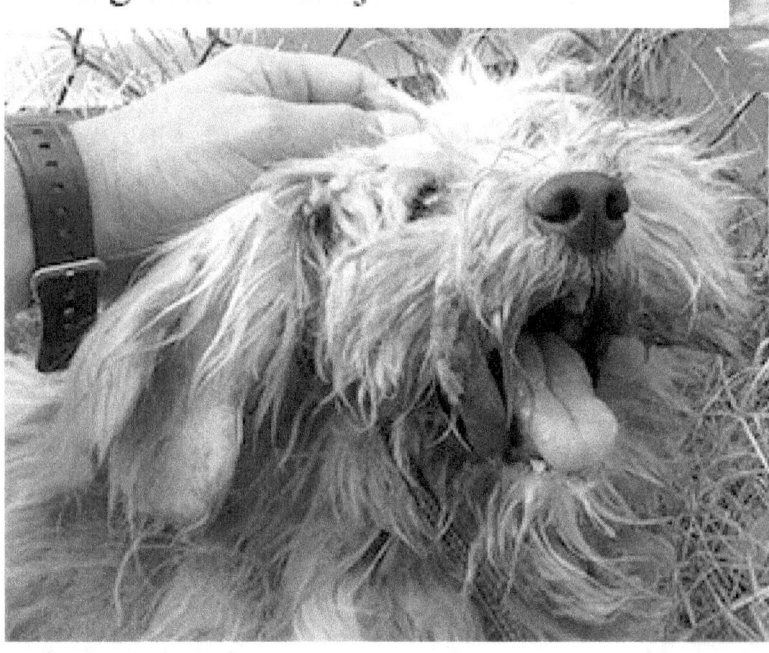

"My ducky!"

A happy home and new friend.

A new haircut and a warm spot.

Bethany - On the brink of Death

Hope For Paws was contacted concerning a stray shepherd mix about a year old on the brink of death. Desperately in need of medical care Bethany may not survive even with the help of Hope For Paws. That still did not stop Eldad from trying to save her. Catching her was not going to be an issue because she could barely move. Bethany just laid there when Hope For Paws arrived. It was difficult to tell if she was even alive. Her paws were so swollen from infection, making it very painful for her to stand, but Bethany still stood up and advanced to Eldad's comforting hands. A little spooked at first Bethany started limping away but Eldad's assistant was able to catch her attention with a tasty cheeseburger. While Bethany nibbled on the treat they carefully placed the Hope For Paws lucky leash around her neck. They then loaded her into the back of the car and Bethany snuggled up in some blankets. On the way to the vet Bethany made her way into the front seat insisting on cuddling with her rescuers.

Dr. Erin Wilson examined Bethany. She was extremely dehydrated and had severe mange. Bethany also suffered numerous infections that included her eyes, bladder, and four others through-out her body. Her skin was raw and covered mostly in scabs, missing most of her fur. She also had recently miscarried a litter of puppies due to her poor health. First things first she received a nice warm medicated bath. Even though it was painful, Bethany accepted the soak and the attention knowing it was helping. She spent the next few weeks on I.V. antibiotics at the hospital. While there the team spent every free moment they could to help mend her spirit and her body. Today you would not even recognize Bethany. Although her fur may never grow back completely she is still beautiful. Weighing about 50 pounds she is the perfect snuggling size and loves every minute of it. Bethany is incredibly smart and has picked up training very quickly. She is affectionate, playful, and loves other dogs.

After 23 days at the hospital Bethany was finally able to go to her foster home while she awaited adoption. Daily antibiotic injections continued, but while there Bethany became best friends with her new furry companion who helped mend her soul even further. Both Bethany and her canine soul mate were adopted together and are happily living it up in their lovin

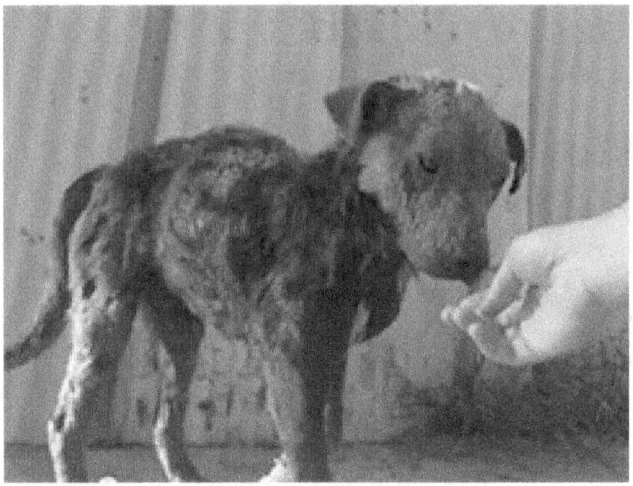

Bethany during the rescue.

I just need some time to heal.

On her way to a better life with her new friend.

Bethany is such a beautiful baby.

Brutus - The gentle giant

Hope For Paws received a call about a one-and-a-half-year-old pit bull who had been living on the streets of downtown Los Angeles for a few months. He was so ready to be saved that he walked right up to Eldad and Lisa Arturo. Brutus had been living in a mechanic's lot getting food from the workers. The mechanics felt it was time for Brutus to find a loving home and contacted Hope For Paws. Brutus was the easiest rescue they ever had, taking only 10 minutes. The gentle giant followed Lisa and Eldad to their car sporting the Hope For Paws lucky leash and jumped right on Lisa's lap. The entire ride to the vet Brutus gave both his new friends hugs and sloppy kisses thanking them the only way he knew how. However, Lisa and Eldad did not mind. The trio drove past some graffiti, "Don't worry everything is going to be amazing." It was the perfect sign to a perfect rescue.

Brutus was underweight and suffered from a flea infestation but was in overall good health. This was amazing considering he had been on the streets for so long. He was given his vaccinations and Lisa gave him a warm bath to wash away the horrors of his previous life.

Brutus was adopted by a family with children and is living it up in his new forever loving home. To this day Brutus and Lisa still have a beautiful bond, and he will always have a place in her heart. Pit bulls are often given a bad name, but Brutus was proof that it is not the breed that is the problem. Many aggressive pit bulls become that way out of fear from abuse and neglect. Though Brutus had suffered both, he still has love in his heart and the need for companionship.

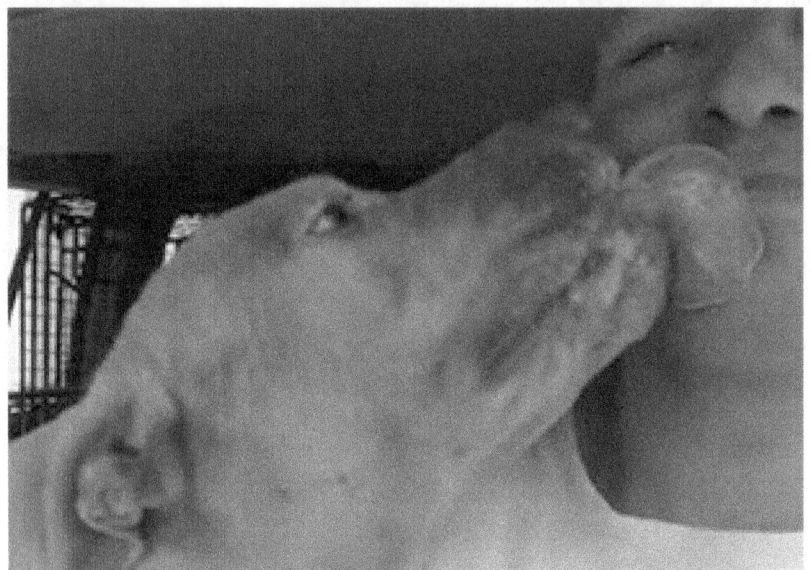

Sloppy kisses for Eldad

What a handsome baby

Friends Fur-ever

Buddha - He just needed a hug and a cheeseburger

Hope For Paws received an urgent call about a large stray three-year-old pit bull in South Central Los Angeles. He was living in an abandoned lot struggling to survive. The neighborhood children had been abusing Buddha by throwing rocks at him. This resulted in a painful abscess the size of a fist on his shoulder. Contrary to his humongous size, he was scared and in desperate need of emotional healing. This giant sweetheart cowered behind a recycle bin as Eldad attempted to move closer. To gain his trust, Eldad spoke kind words and offered a jumbo cheeseburger. Buddha instantly took the tasty treat and swallowed it whole. Eldad went behind the chain link fence and gently placed the Hope For Paws lucky leash around Buddha's neck. He immediately stood up and slowly followed Eldad to the car. All in all, it took about an hour of bonding until Buddha was ready to leave with Eldad. The entire ride to the vet Buddha laid his head on Eldad's chest and fell asleep. This was the most peace he ever had, and his journey to recovery was just beginning.

At the vet, Buddha received all the medical attention he needed. He was bathed, giving a flea dip, and treated for his infections. He was then able to receive surgery on his shoulder to remove the giant abscess. Luckily it was a great success.

While at his foster home, Buddha became inseparable best friends with a kitty named Fierro. They loved each other so much, that their foster parents insisted they be adopted into their forever home together.

If not for the help of Hope For Paws and the compassion of donors like yourselves, Buddha may have succumbed to his injuries, more abuse, and starvation. Even worse, he could have been picked up by animal control and deemed a lost cause resulting in euthanasia.

Buddha hiding in an empty lot, not knowing how much his life is about to change for the better.

"Can I has more cheeseburger?"

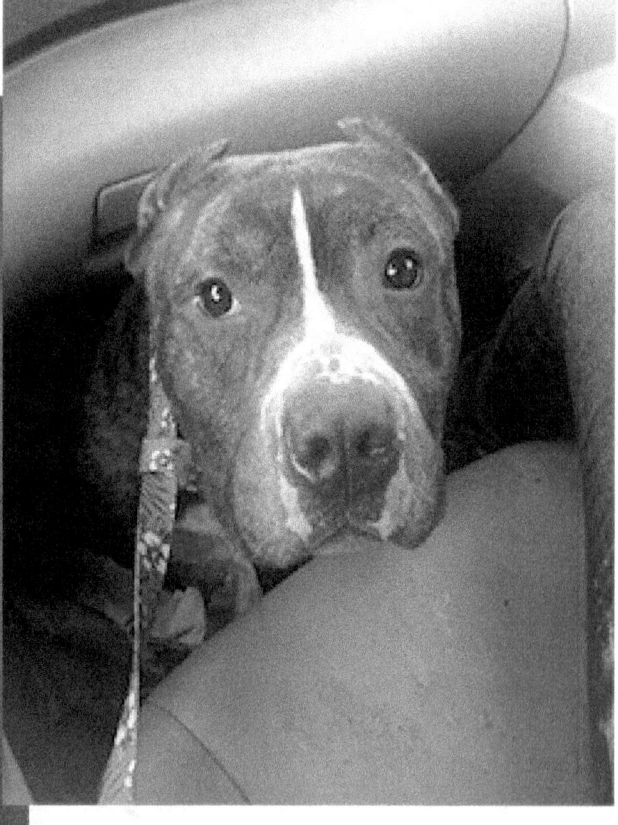

Brothers from another mother.

Cadence – The sweetest creature on this planet

Eldad received an urgent call from some of Lisa Chiarelli's friends regarding a pit bull who was wandering the streets of Los Angeles. Lisa's friends informed her that they had followed Cadence for two hours until she had finally collapsed inside a dark alleyway. When Eldad found Cadence she was lying on the ground barely moving. Her head hung low, Cadence was in immense pain and anyone could see that. Talking softly to her, Eldad gently placed the Hope For Paws lucky leash around her neck. Cadence accepted Eldad's loving touch. She slowly stood up and they made their way to Eldad's car and onto Hollywood where she could get the medical attention she so desperately needed.

Cadence's face was extremely swollen and it was apparent that she was used as a bait dog as part of a dog fighting ring. This was a life this sweetheart did not deserve. Her pain was over now and a loving home awaited Cadence. She required surgery on her face to reduce the swelling from her injuries. She also required a second surgery to save her eyes. Thanks to Dr. Christin Fahrer it was a success. 24 hours after surgery Cadence had already improved greatly. She gave kisses and wagged her tail, sharing love to everyone she met. The day after her rescue Hope For Paws saved another pit bull named Chance who was also a victim of a dog fighting ring. Cadence and Chance became inseparable, it was love at first sight. Chance eased Cadence's pain by kissing her wounds. Cadence had a new lease on life and plenty of loving friends to show her how beautiful the world truly is.

At her new foster home with Lisa, Cadence learned to swim and trust humans again. She is wonderful with other dogs and gentle around children. Cadence was adopted into a loving family in Southern California and even has her own Facebook page! Eldad and Lisa visit her frequently f or sloppy puppy kisses.

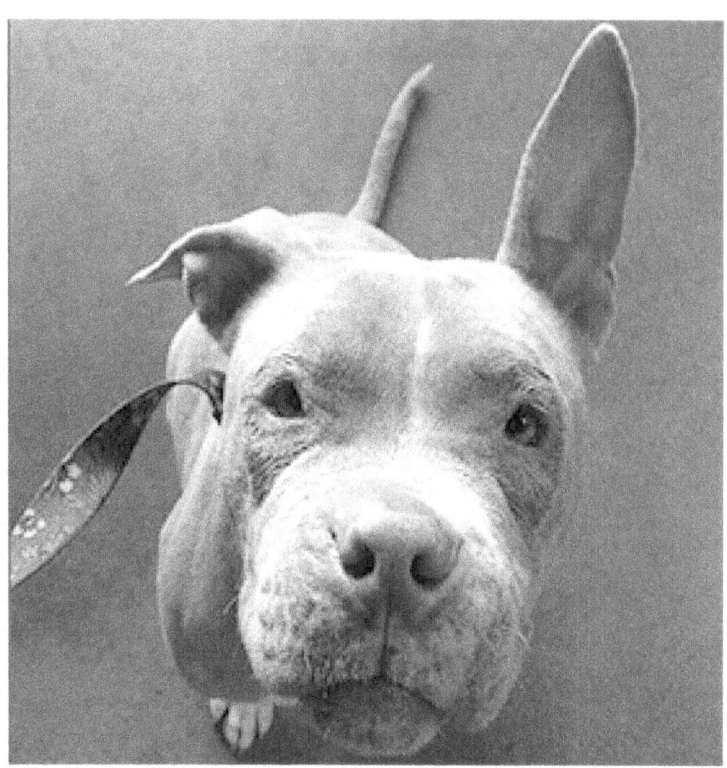

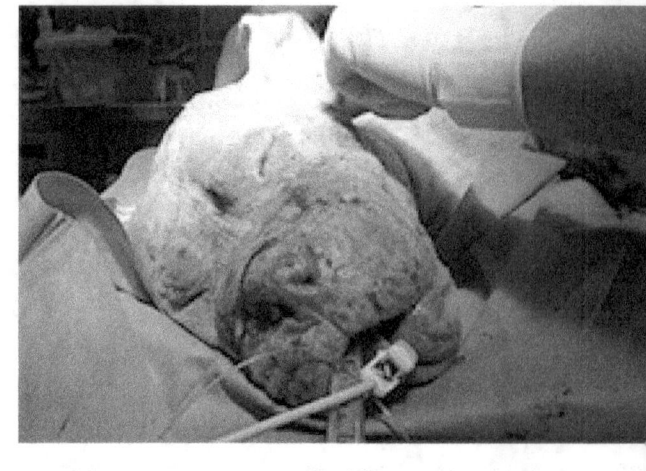

Lost and alone, but not for long.

We will make you feel better baby gir

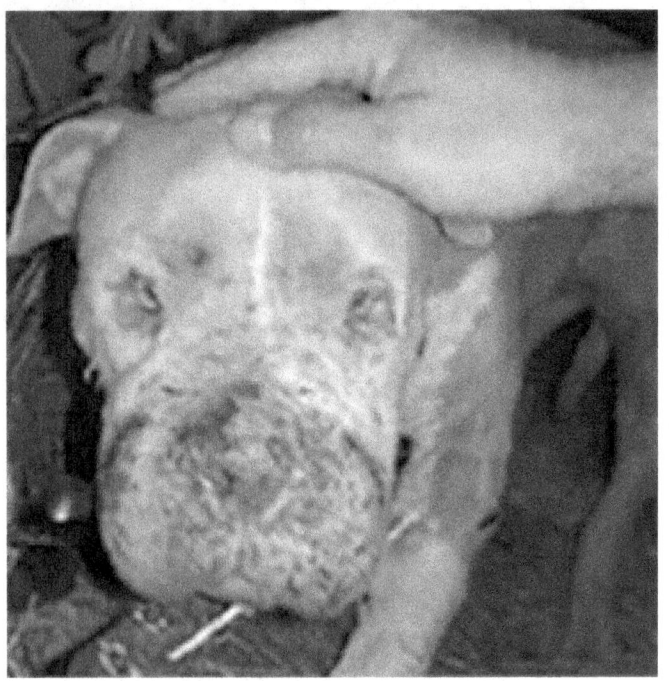

Puppy love.

Cadence giving Eldad love

Clarabelle - The loving touch

This would be Hope For Paws fifth attempt at locating a homeless one year old golden retriever. They had received tips about the dog wandering the industrial section of Los Angeles. Finally, Eldad and Lisa Arturo spotted Clarabelle running under a shipping container. It was apparent that thiswas not going to be an easy rescue. Eldad along with his gentle snare climbed under the container that Clarabelle had hid under. After what seemed like forever he finally had her on his leash. Clarabelle became immediately upset rolling around on the ground whining. As she laid on her back frozen in fear with her paws over her eyes, Eldad tried to comfort her. He grew the courage to pet her and she soaked it up. This was obviously the first in a long time since she had felt a loving touch. Eldad had no other choice but to carefully pull her out from under the container. Once outside Clarabelle did a complete 180 and began snuggling her rescuers as they petted her. Eldad then placed the Hope For Paws lucky leash around Clarabelle's neck, and Lisa carried her to their car. Then on to the vet they went.

Hope For Paws gave her a much-needed bath, vital medical care, and immunizations.

Clarabelle is now a happy goof ball which Goldens are famous for.

What sets Hope For Paws apart from the rest is the time they take to earn the dog's trust. In this case, it took four hours under that shipping container for Eldad to comfort Clarabelle to the point where she was no longer terrified. Building a relationship from the first meeting is ground work for rehabilitating a frightened animal like Clarabelle. It is also for the dog and the rescuers safety to not traumatize the animal any more than it already is.

This poor sweetheart was terrified beyond belief.

A loving touch is sometimes all its takes.

Freedom in the arms of her rescuer.

Clarabelle is one happy puppy.

Edie - The second chance

In March 2010 Hope For Paws received a call from a friend who told him about Edie, a beautiful 10 pound Maltese who was scheduled to be euthanized the next day. Eldad's friend could not let that happen and contacted Hope For Paws for help. Edie had been at the Lancaster Animal Shelter, a high kill shelter for over two weeks. Deemed too aggressive for adoption, she was to be euthanized. Edie was not violent, but terrified from a lifetime of abuse and neglect. All she needed was someone to show her what love was. Eldad took the challenge and headed to the shelter to rescue her. At the shelter Eldad lifted the top off Edie's cage, and she immediately started growling at him. The poor thing was covered in dirty matted fur. Her fur was so out of control you could not even see her eyes. She backed herself into a corner, and Eldad approached cautiously with the Hope For Paws lucky leash. Successfully getting the leash around her neck, Edie was so terrified she defecated on the floor. Eldad pulled her onto his lap and she immediately surrendered. All she really needed was a hug. Within seconds Edie became a different dog. She soaked up all the petting and comforting words that Eldad offered her. They spent an hour together cuddling and bonding while Eldad made sure she understood he was there to help. Finally, the first tail wag and a roll over for a belly rub showed Eldad that his trust had been earned. It was time to go to the vet to begin healing her body and the rest of her soul.

At the vet, Edie received a much-needed bath and shaving to remove her matts. She ran through the office wagging her tail at the loss of that dirty weight from years of neglect. After 6 days at the vet she was ready to go to her new foster home in San Marino, California. When Edie met her foster family, she Eskimo kissed her new mommy hello. That very person who just so happened to be the same woman who originally called Eldad for help in getting Edie out of the pound. Six months later, Edie's foster family successfully adopted her.

There are so many dogs in kill shelters across the globe who need our help. They are the most grateful, loving creatures on this planet. Before you go to a pet store, stop by your local pound and see who is there. You never know, you just might find who you are really looking for, or they may find you.

Edie is Ready for her healing
to begin.

"Do I look pretty yet?"

It's okay Edie it's only temporary your
beautiful locks will grow back.

Hank - The old man on the mountain

Everyone needs a little vacation, but for Hope For Paws their work never truly takes a break. On their second trip to Costa Rica, Eldad and his team visited their old friend Scott Alan Bradley, founder of the Costa Rica dog and rescue Adoption center. A gorgeous free range animal rescue center nestled in the jungles of La Fortuna. During their stay Eldad and Lisa Chiarelli, along with Scott were able to rescue and rehabilitate 10 dogs. Costa Rica is riddled with strays and due to the abundant exotic wildlife, it is not safe for these domestic creatures to survive in the wild.

The sun had set after a long day and it was time for the team to finally settle down and enjoy a nice warm meal. Or so they thought. When Eldad heard Scott yell for help, he stepped outside and found Lisa feeding what they believed was a Sharpei mix. Hank, as they would name him, allowed Lisa to place the Hope For Paws lucky leash around his neck. Believed to be around 8 years old, Hank was in bad shape. His face was swollen from cuts. He was bleeding all over. More shocking than his appearance was the fact that this old man knew to come to the compound for help. Believed to have been attacked by another animal. Hank had trekked the long journey up the mountain, somehow knowing that he would find the help he needed. Inside Eldad called the vet but it was too late in the evening. The only thing they could do was make Hank as comfortable and loved as possible until the morning. The next day Hank was in good spirits as he wagged his tail and gave nuzzles to everyone at the center.

The team wasted no time in getting Hank to the vet. Upon examination, Hank was diagnosed with several infections from his wounds and a poor appetite while struggling to survive in the wild. He also tested positive for heartworms and needed to be hospitalized. During his stay at the hospital Hank made many new furry friends, each day they greeted Hank from his window in hopes of cheering the old man up.

After a few weeks Hank was finally well enough to travel. Scott and Hank hopped on a plane and headed to Los Angeles to reunite him with the Hope For Paws team.

The wonderful people at Grand Paws Rescue in Los Angeles offered to take Hank into their foster care. While he still requires medication to cure his heartworms, Hank is in great health considering his age. Thanks to the help of Nancy and the rest of the Grand Paws rescue team, Hank is enjoying his comfortable new life. While he is still waiting for his loving forever home, Hank is in the best care possible and loving his new life at Grand Paws Rescue.

Lisa made a new friend tonight.

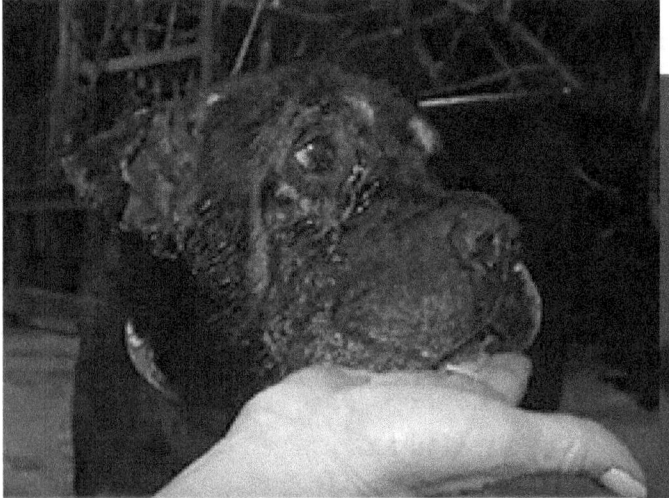

Poor baby, you'll feel better soon.

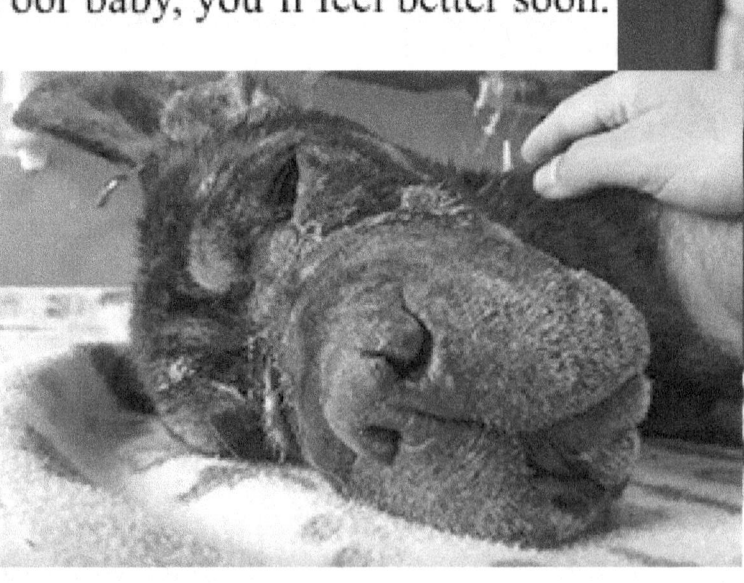

What a handsome boy.

Holly - All you need is love

When a concerned citizen reached out to Hope For Paws about an abandoned dog, Eldad had no clue of the pain he was about to witness. They pulled up in front of a home and saw a tiny Terrier Chihuahua mix huddled on the porch, shivering in fear. Holly would be her name and she needed immediate emotional help. Eldad tried calming her down with pieces of chicken but Holly was not interested, she was too terrified. Eldad resorted to using his catch pole because she was being very aggressive. Holly attacked the gentle snare, barking, growling, and then retreated to her corner to hide. Once Eldad finally got her in his snare she continued to fight. He took a blanket, gently stroking her head to calm the poor soul down. After about 20 minutes Holly finally realized that Eldad was only there to help. She allowed him to put her on his lap and place the Hope For Paws lucky leash around her neck. She rested her head against his chest and trembled as Eldad stroked her fur. Holly had a long way to rehabilitation, but she was in loving hands now.

At the vet, Holly received the Hope For Paws treatment. They made sure she was spayed and vaccinated. Then she received a nice warm bath. She was in good health but the emotional damage would take more than just one trip to the Doctor to fix. Holly needed a loving family to pull her out of her shell.

Three weeks later Holly was placed into a foster home and has made great progress. Playing with her new pack and foster family has helped her to heal. Eventually Holly was adopted along with her fellow rescue buddy Wally. They are now living a peaceful life in their new forever loving home.

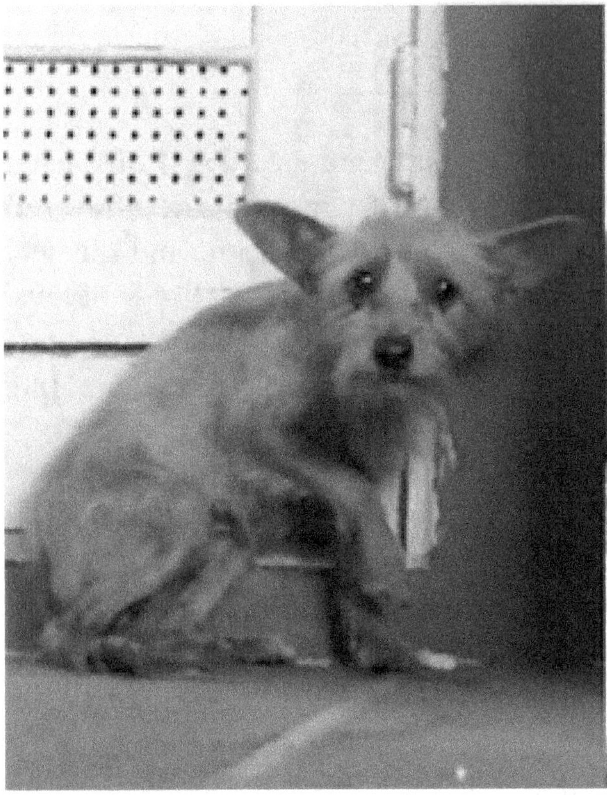

It will be okay now baby girl.

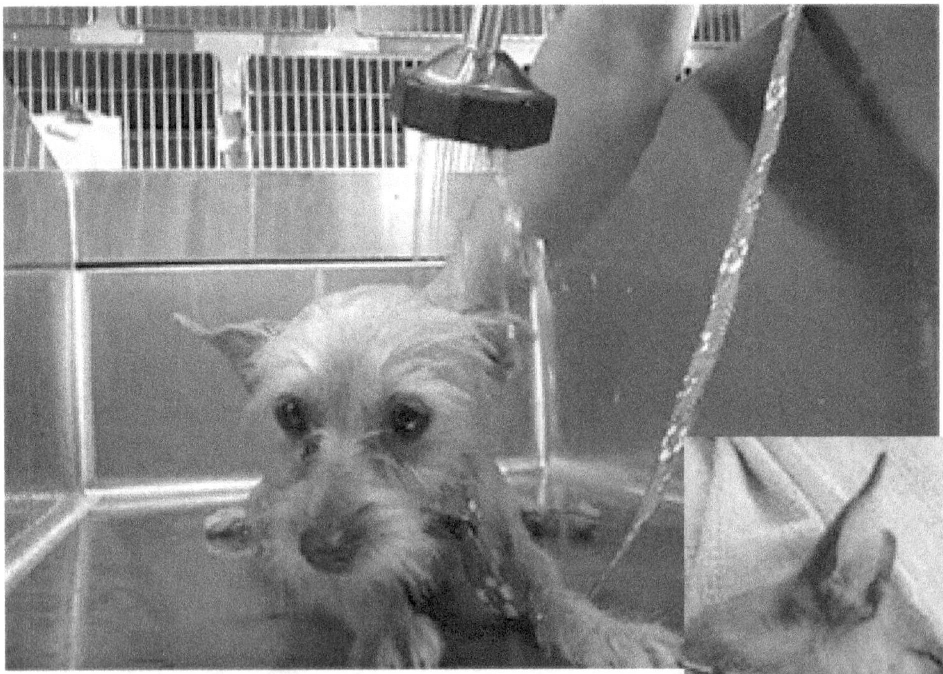

Washing away the pain.

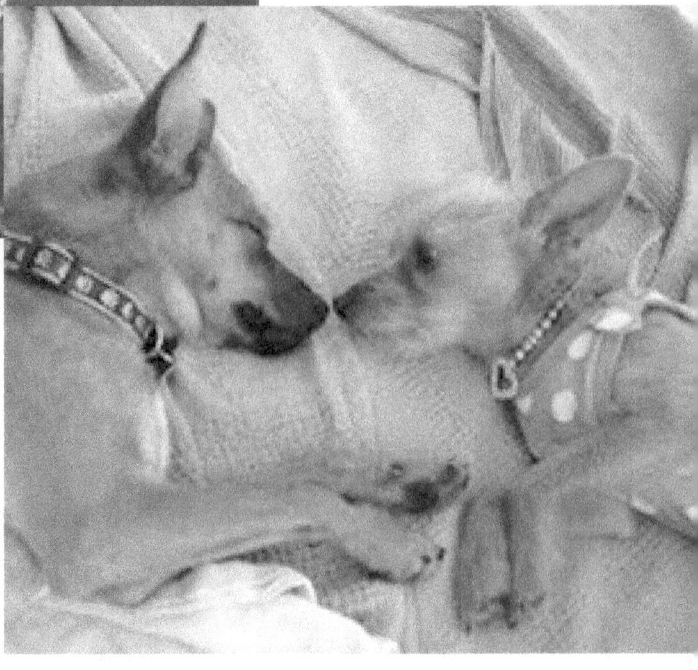

New friendship.

Jordan - The little miracle

Hope For Paws received an emergency call for help. Volunteers from L.A. on Cloud 9 had spotted a puppy trapped inside the Los Angeles river. An on looker told Eldad that the dog had been brutally abused by a homeless man and then thrown 30 feet down into the canal. Eldad had no clue what he was about to witness. Huddled on an empty potato chip bag, in the middle of puddles of filthy algae infested water, Jordan sat. His fur was almost completely gone from a severe case of mange. With head hung low in pain, he could barely move. Eldad soon would discover why the dog was in so much pain. After climbing down the wall into the river, Eldad carefully lifted Jordan to discover that his leg had been cut clean off at the knee. Jordan moaned from the extreme agony of being touched. Eldad placed Jordan inside a crate and Lisa Chiarelli lifted him up the wall and into the car.

They rushed Jordan to the vet. The doctor said it was a miracle he was still alive. He suffered from mange, a bacterial infection, and malnutrition. He also required surgery to remove what was left of his back leg. Jordan received multiple blood transfusions thanks to the donation from Laila, another rescue from earlier that week. He required sedation each time his bandage needed changing, making sure he was as comfortable as possible. Jordan was a super star and everyone at the clinic was rooting for his survival. After four days Jordan finally felt well enough to have surgery on his leg. The surgery was a success and a few days later Jordan was well enough to go home with foster mommy Lisa. Left with only 3 legs that did not slow Jordan down. With every passing day he grew stronger. His fur grew back and the puppy inside was as playful as any other four-legged canine.

While living with Lisa, Jordan made many new friends including chickens, and of course Lisa's pack Lola and Frankie. Daily rehabilitation exercises strengthened Jordan's legs, there was no stopping this sweetheart. Against the odds, he survived and now has the love he deserves. Jordan has been adopted in his loving forever home, and the horrors of his past are nothing more than ghosts. He may have lost his leg, but Jordan never lost hope.

No way to start a life.

All puppy!

"Hope For Paws fixered me up."

Best friends fur-eve

Julia - The loving wolf hybrid

Hope For Paws received a text message from a woman who had spotted what looked like a wolf hybrid wandering the streets of Los Angeles. The photo the woman included left Eldad stricken with sadness. Julia, who was believed to be around 2 years old was dying. Eldad and Lisa Chiarelli jumped into their car and rushed to Julia's rescue. As luck would have it, Julia had wandered into a fenced yard so that Eldad could shut the gate and secure her inside. As they approached Julia the situation was worse than they could ever imagine. The sweet dog was extremely swollen from infections that covered her entire body. She was bleeding. There was pus oozing everywhere and it is hard to see from the photos, but Julia was nothing but skin and bones. Apparently she was previously owned as a ratty rope was wrapped tightly around her neck. Julia was an abuse case and neglected at a criminal level. Wary of her human rescuers, Julia carefully approached Lisa and gently accepted the tasty cheeseburger. It took 20 minutes for Julia to finally allow Lisa to place the Hope For Paws lucky leash on her. The trio hopped in the car and rushed Julia to the vet. There was no time to waste, she needed to be treated before her infections caused permanent damage.

At the vet the state of Julia's abuse and neglect became apparent. A series of tests showed that she was suffering from a severe form of mange causing her hair loss and inflamed skin. Her nails were so long that they had begun curling up into the pads of her paws, making it incredibly difficult for her to walk. Julia was given a medicated bath that exposed even more horrors. As the warm water hit her it began breaking down her scabs causing Julia to bleed everywhere. The water that ran off of her was filled with puss, dirt, fleas, and blood. Even through all the pain and confusion Julia understood that Hope For Paws was there to save her and accepted their love. She rested her head on Lisa's chest who warmed her with a towel. After all the pain Julia endured that day it was finally time to lie down and begin healing. Julia was tucked into a cozy blanket and fell asleep. The next day Julia had already showed improvement. She began eating to regain her strength and became affectionate by nuzzling her new two legged friends.

Julia's recovery will take time as her body and mind need to heal from years of unknown terror that she had experienced. Over the next few days Julia's health took a turn for the worst again. The infections started causing fevers and a loss of appetite. She was getting the best care possible at the hospital. It was just going to take a little more time for her to mend.

With the love and determination of Hope For Paws and Julia's strong spirit, she finally was healthy enough to be placed into a foster home. At her new loving home, Julia became part of the pack and is enjoying her second chance at life with her two new wolf hybrid siblings.

On the mend.

Underneath all that filth is a beautiful creature.

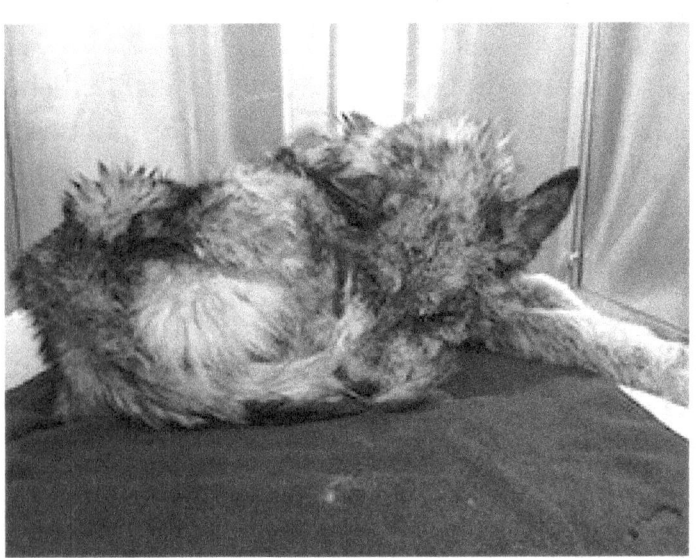

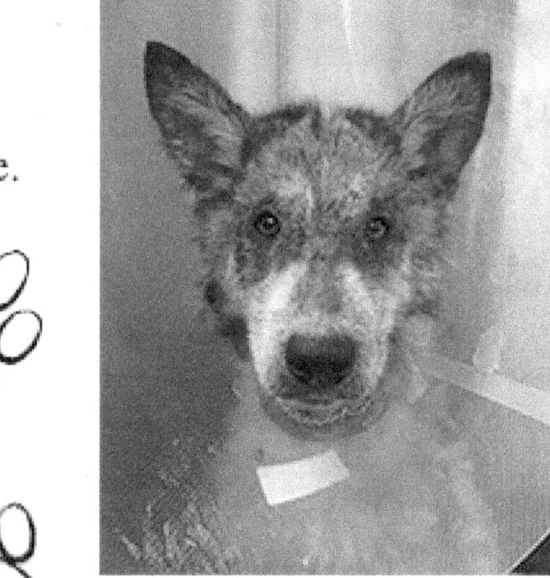

A toasty warm bath.

There is that gorgeous girl.

Kayla - The littlest puppy with the biggest heart

In Tijuana, Mexico lived a puppy named Kayla. She was abused by a true monster, and her story is one filled with horror and sadness. When Hope For Paws got a call concerning a puppy in need, they had no idea that it would be the worst case of animal abuse the team had ever seen. A volunteer traveled down to Mexico to retrieve the sweet soul and bring her back to Eldad in hopes of saving her. Kayla suffered from a tick disease that was shutting down her immune system, as well as intestinal parasites. The most horrific of her injuries was that someone had stabbed her left eye out and cut off her front leg. It would take a miracle to save this little pooch, but she was a fighter. The sweetheart suffered so much pain, it was truly astounding that she still had love in her heart for humans. She knew the Hope For Paws team was there to save her.

Kayla would not be able to have surgery for a few days after she got to California. Her immune system was too weak to risk the operation. Her body was extremely frail from fighting off all the infections. Even with all her discomfort she still was able to give the team love and affection, wagging her tail and licking her rescuers as they bathed her wounds. Finally, they were able to remove what was left of her right eye and her left leg. She began healing and despite the horrific cruelty she is the sweetest love bug, and the definition of never giving up.

Kayla was adopted by her own personal vet tech at the Hope For Paws Veterinary Care center. During the day she accompanies her new mommy to the hospital for more I.V. Fluids. Each night she goes home to a nice warm comfortable bed, and a loving family.

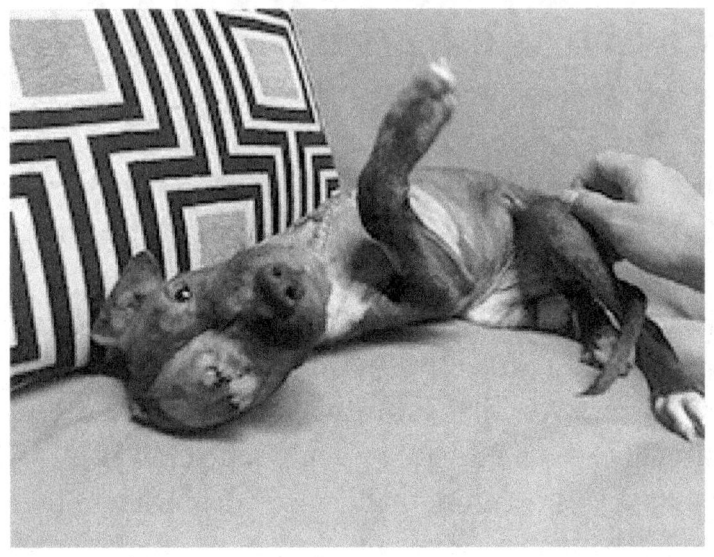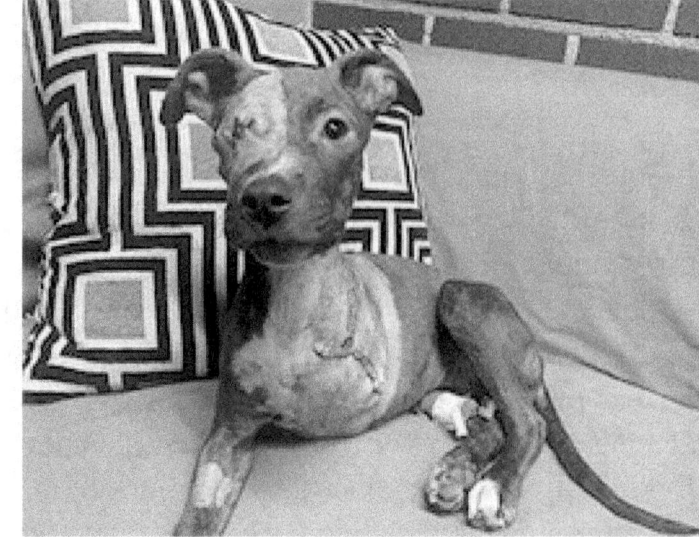

Well on her way to recovery.

Three legs don't slow this puppy down.

A beautiful soul.

Lexus, Mercedes, Cooper, Beamer and Prius
From rags to riches

Eldad had received an urgent plea for help about a 5-year-old stray pit bull who had just given birth in someone's yard. Eldad did not hesitate to rush to their rescue. Lisa Arturo and Monica set up a yellow netted fence so that Lexus, the mommy could not escape. Eldad approached slowly to test her temperament. As with any other animal, a mother can be very protective of her children, so Eldad had to advance carefully. It was night time and it made it very difficult to find the puppies hidden in the bushes. Neighbors volunteered to surround the fence, to keep Lexus from breaking through and escaping. It took a few moments but Eldad finally was able to restrain Lexus using his gentle snare. She was relieved to feel the touch of a loving hand. The next step was to help the newborn puppies. Eldad found them behind a tree, they were so young that their eyes were not even open yet. Sadly, one of the puppies did not make it. Eldad wrapped him up in a blanket to take him back to Hope For Paws and give the poor little guy a proper farewell. Lexus' other four puppies were carefully placed inside a towel lined crate. The whole family headed to Eldad's car and on to the Veterinary Care Center.

Lexus and her puppies were all infested with fleas and given soothing warm baths. Mommy Lexus tried to help Lisa dry them off with her tongue. After the babies nursed, Lexus placed her paw on Eldad's knee and starting whining. She was trying to tell him something was wrong. They quickly took an x-ray of Lexus' stomach only to find a bottle cap was lodged inside her tummy. Not wanting to perform surgery on a nursing mother, they decided to induce vomiting in hopes of removing the cap. Lexus was given some medication and she immediately regurgitated the bottle cap on the first try! The entire family was given a clean bill of health and the next day they went on to their foster home. There they would live until the puppies were old enough to be adopted.

On Thanksgiving night 2014, Lexus and her puppies appeared on Fox's "Cause for Paws: An All-Star Dog Spectacular." The show was to promote awareness for other dog's in Lexus' situation. A-list stars such as Channing Tatum, Scarlett Johansson, Jane Lynch, Pink and many many more attended to support the cause. However, Lexus, Mercedes, Cooper, Beamer and Prius were the ones who stole the spotlight.

Lexus and everyone of her puppies were adopted. Lexus or Lexi for short, has found a loving forever home with a beautiful couple. She is enjoying every moment of her peaceful second chance at happiness.

"It's okay mama we are here to take you home."

A warm bath, some hungry puppies and wait, what is that? A bottle cap!

From rags to riches.

One beautiful family

Miley - The forgotten one

Hope For Paws received an urgent call about a sick dog living in a trash dump. As Eldad walked up to her he could not believe what he saw. There laid the most beautiful husky and malamute mix puppy, not even a year old. She was dying on a filthy old mattress, the only bed she had ever known. Huskies are notoriously joyful, giant goof balls of fluff, but there was no happiness to be seen in this sweetheart's eyes. She was in agony, in desperate need of medical help. Miley's ribs were sticking out from starvation. You could smell the stench of rot rolling off of her body from the mange. Eldad spent over an hour in that trash pile caressing Miley, speaking comforting words to earn her trust. He gently laid the Hope For Paws lucky leash around her neck and Miley slowly got up after some tasty cheeseburger. She hesitantly followed Eldad to his vehicle but then hopped in. As they began their trip to the Veterinary Care Center, she rested her head on Eldad. He caressed her as he told the sweet beauty everything was going to be alright.

Miley suffered from mange, bloody sores, parasites, a 105-degree fever, bacterial infections, severe malnutrition, and dehydration. She needed medicated baths and treatments for all of her wounds. Miley was shut down and needed time to heal. Lisa Arturo gave Miley her first warm bath and cuddled the sweet baby. It took three days but she finally gained enough strength to thank Eldad with loving kisses.

Miley was taken into foster care and after over 500 adoption applications she was finally adopted into a loving forever home. To this day Eldad still visits her regularly as she will always be a part of his heart and soul.

Forgotten and alone.

Miley is a fighter.

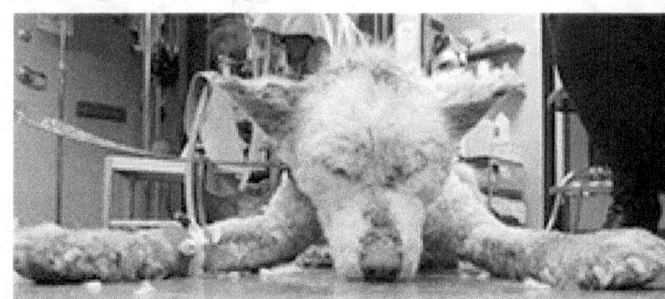

It's time to go hom
sweetheart.

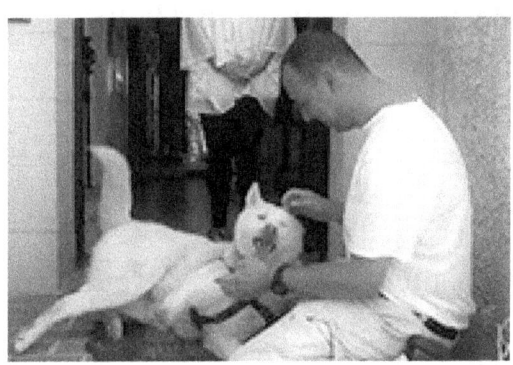

Such a beautiful baby.

A year later and Miley is
over joyed to see Eldad.

Forever in each others hearts.

Mufasa - The handsome old man

Hope For Paws received a call about an abandoned 8-year-old husky mix, that had been living in a water treatment facility. Mufasa was dangerously close to the open tanks containing hazardous chemicals. It was going to take some careful maneuvering to capture the old boy in these conditions. Lisa Arturo threw bits of cheeseburger to lure him closer. However, the terrified old man was reluctant to get close. It would take some time before Mufasa would become comfortable enough to place the gentle snare on him. After years of living on the streets, unfortunately he would not calm down. Eldad was forced to take other measures. Climbing up the stairs to the platform behind Mufasa, Eldad was able to place the leash around his neck, which Mufasa was none too happy about. He immediately began tossing around and urinated out of fear. Mufasa, although shaken up was safe now and in good hands. Sporting the Hope For Paws lucky leash, Mufasa followed the team to their car and onwards to a new and better life. On the ride to the vet Mufasa sat up front with Eldad, gobbling up more tasty cheeseburgers and giving Eldad kisses.

Mufasa smelled like a sewer and his skin was in bad shape. A nice warm medicated bath to wash away the filth and grime would fix him right up. The old man was also neutered, microchipped, vaccinated, treated for an ear infection, and intestinal parasites.

Mufasa was taken to his new foster home and has become the sweetest thing. He is like a puppy now, and is so happy to be alive and well. He eventually was adopted into a loving forever home. Along with the love of his new furry brother and sister, Mufasa is enjoying his second chance at a peaceful and joyful new life.

Waiting for a miracle.

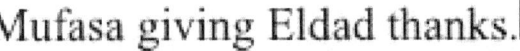

Mufasa giving Eldad thanks.

Such a gorgeous
old man.

Petunia and Petals – The little lost family

Petunia had been living alone on the streets for months, surviving off the scraps from good samaritans at a nearby park. When Hope For Paws heard about the stray, Lisa Arturo and Eldad headed straight out to save the sweet little soul. Finding her wandering around a parking lot of a nursery, she hid under a parked pickup truck. Eldad crawled under the vehicle, Petunia although frightened wagged her tail showing Eldad that his help was appreciated. Eldad took hold of Petunia and pulled her out from under the truck, and onto his lap. She sat there soaking up the affection. As he rubbed her belly Eldad noticed that Petunia was lactating, she had recently given birth to puppies. Now the hunt began to find her babies. It did not take very long for the team to find a single puppy, who was hiding in a pile of leaves nearby. Petals the puppy was only 3 days old and had not even opened her eyes yet. Eldad was worried that Petunia may have hidden more puppies elsewhere. He used a handy little trick to get Petunia to bring him to the rest of the litter. Firstly, he placed the Hope For Paws lucky leash on her, so that she could not run off on him. He turned his phone on YouTube and a played a video of crying puppies. Sure enough the sound made Petunia's maternal instincts kick in, and she headed towards where the puppies were. She continued to go back to the spot where they found Petals, the team realized that Petunia only had one puppy left.

Eldad and Lisa along with their new furry friends headed straight to the vet. With only an ear infection in her, she was given a clean bill of health. Soon after Petals was old enough for solid foods, Petunia was spayed.

The little lost family is now enjoying their new happy lives in their forever loving homes.

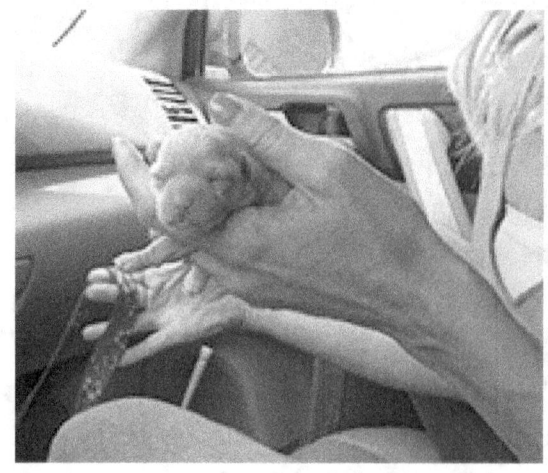

It's okay Petunia we are going to take you home.   Little Miss Petals.

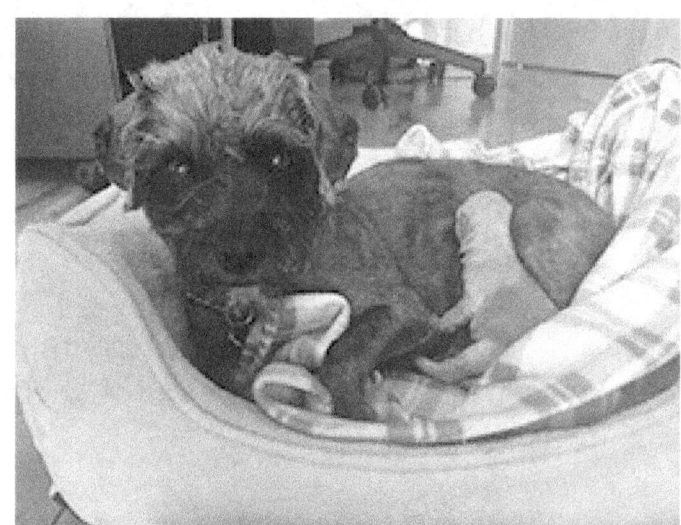

A cozy bed for Momma and Baby.

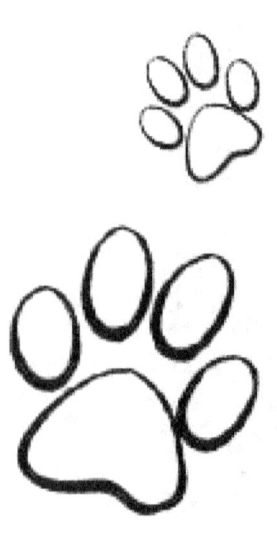

Tinkerbell - If you love someone they'll come back to you

While most of Hope For Paws rescues seem to be that of only homeless and abandoned dogs, sometimes a lost family member can need Hope For Paws assistance as well.

Fourth of July weekend a family from Arizona was visiting Los Angeles. The neighborhood children were outside playing with little fireworks. The fireworks were loud enough to spook the family's beloved pet Tinkerbell, a 10-year-old 110-pound Mastiff. Tinkerbell jumped the fence and took off, ending up more than 25 miles away to Santa Monica from her vacation spot in Compton, and her worried family. The gentle giant plunged 20 feet into the Los Angeles river, fracturing her leg on the way down. For three months the family hunted for Tinkerbell, to no avail. Finally, a local woman noticed Tinkerbell limping around inside the ravine and immediately called Hope For Paws for help. Eldad and Lisa Arturo reached the spot where Tinkerbell ended up, just a few feet from where the river meets the Pacific Ocean. This would be no easy task to get this massive puppy up and out of her prison. Eldad climbed down his ladder into the river and began doing what he does best, earning Tinkerbell's trust. She was terrified at first, charging at Eldad and Lisa, barking, and growling. Eldad managed to get her with his gentle snare, unfortunately it landed around her muzzle, making it easy for her to get lose. Instead of trying to readjust it he used a second one to place safely around her neck securing her. Eldad and Lisa placed Tinkerbell inside a massive kennel making it simpler to get her up and over the bridge. Concerned on lookers who had been cheering the team on, had called the Los Angeles Fire Department. They assisted Eldad and Lisa in finally pulling the goliath to freedom. Once Tinkerbell and the Hope For Paws team got inside their vehicle, Tinkerbell opened up to her rescuers and showed them how truly sweet of a dog she was.

At the vet, Tinkerbell was treated for her fractured leg and dehydration. Thankfully she was micro chipped and her family was contacted immediately. Once Tinkerbell was ready, she returned home to her loving family in Arizona.

Never forget to microchip your fur babies, keep your information updated in case of emergency, and make sure to secure your pets on the Fourth of July and New Year's Eve. Even the bravest of animals will get spooked by the loud boom of fireworks.

Trapped with no way out.

Waiting for a miracle

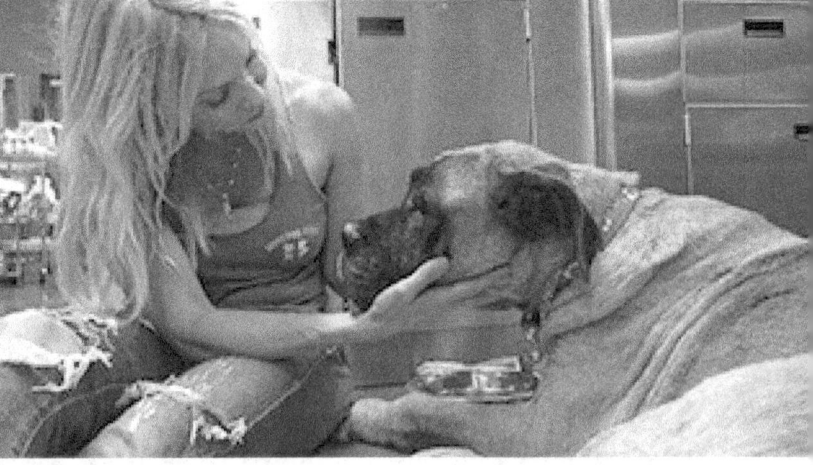

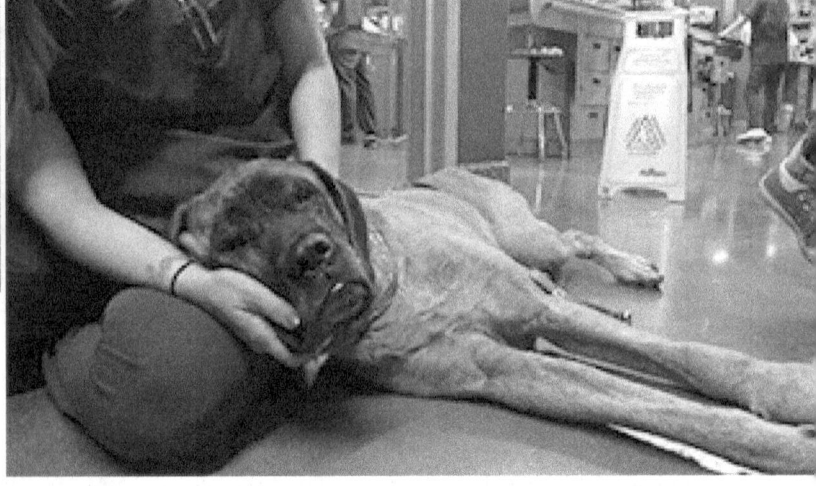

Safe at last, waiting for my
family to take me home.

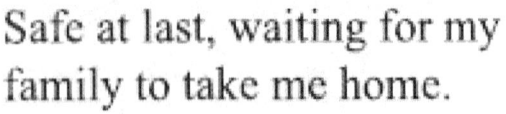

Woody - Waiting for a new love

When Woody's owner died, no arrangements were made to find him a new home. Instead he was abandoned and left to fend for himself out in the cold. Woody waited for over a year, hoping his owner would return. He had been living under a nearby shed, until a good samaritan called Hope For Paws to help the lonely pooch. Woody's hair was so mated and overgrown that it was difficult to see how emaciated his body had become. While neighbors tried to feed him, his heart was what truly needed healing. Hope For Paws arrived to find Woody cowering inside his filthy so called home. It took sometime but Eldad was able to pull Woody out with the gentle snare from underneath the shed and into his lap. From there he began showing Woody the love he so desperately craved. Once outside Lisa Chiarelli placed the Hope For Paws lucky leash on Woody and the trio headed to their car.

At the vet, Woody received more love and affection. He was groomed and given a warm bath. Aside from being extremely underweight, and some damage to his eye, he was in overall good shape. He opened right up to his new two legged friends giving love, nuzzles, and kisses to everyone he met.

Lisa decided to take Woody home into her foster care, there he was surrounded by his new furry friends and a warm place to sleep. He had even regained sight in his right eye. Woody will never have to worry about being abandoned again, now that Hope For Paws has taken him under their wing. After a flood of adoption applications, Woody is now enjoying his comfortable new life in his loving forever home.

Poor little guy.

Waiting for my friend.

Hours later we found a dog under all that fur

Home Sweet Home.

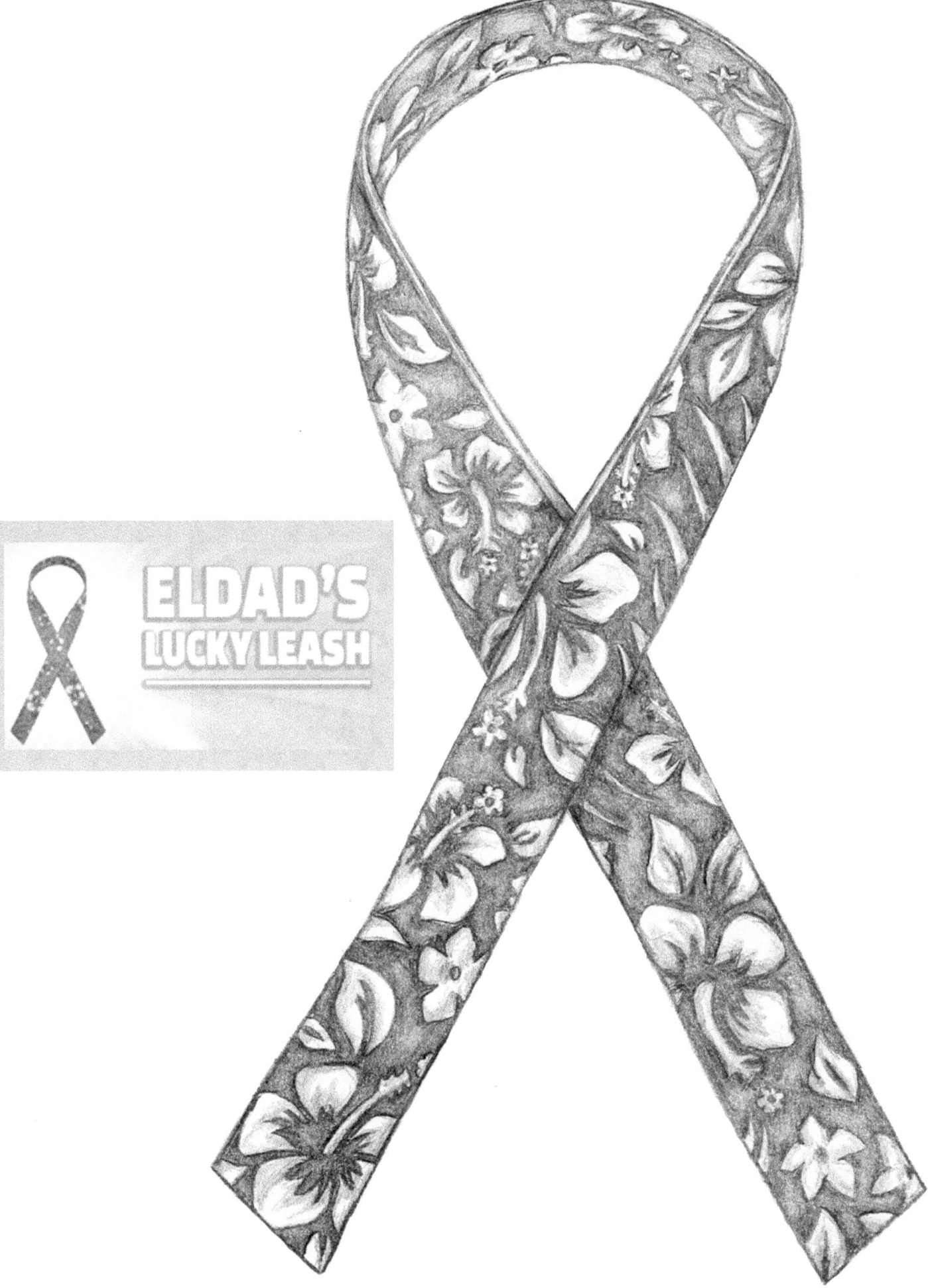

ELDAD'S
LUCKY LEASH